Kisa

A CELEBRATION OF UGANDAN CHILDHOOD

Anne Irene Muyanga

This book is dedicated to my brother **Michael Frederick Mugabi**: Humble intellectual.
I finally took your advice and wrote it! Also, because of you, my life was transformed into
one that sought to give children a better life - a life just like the one we had.

To my brothers:
Henry Stephen Waiswa: Easy going *Shida*.
Dan Ezra Ziraba: Gentle soul.
Emmanuel Musaasizi: Peaceful *Mukagwa*
And to my sister **Sarah Susan Mukoda**: Quiet strength.
Thank you for contributing to the wonderful memories of my childhood.

May You All Rest in Peace.

Uganda,

Home of the source of the River Nile.
A country with green fields of
bananas, sweet potato [embooli], corn, cassava.
Fresh organic mangoes, oranges, groundnuts [amaidho], avocado,
beans and abundant sunshine all year round!

A child growing up in Uganda will surely be
surrounded by love and encouragement from family and
appreciation from the whole village who, collectively,
look out for their best interest.

It is a happy childhood indeed!

The beauty of Uganda can also be seen through the eyes of
people from all corners of the world. They come for a visit and
never want to leave. Others manage to leave only for a
moment and then find themselves back there.

They say they miss the perfectly warm days
and cool evenings; and yes ... the hospitality of
the people.

Sir Winston Churchill aptly summed all this
up into his edict: Uganda - the Pearl of Africa.

Oh Uganda, May God Uphold thee!
Anne Irene Muyanga

ACKNOWLEDGMENTS

Shannon Hart - Reed
A chance encounter not only resurrected an idea that had first been suggested
by my late brother a decade and a half ago; but you also managed to
finally convince me to write this book. As the biggest cheerleader at the start
of this project, you generously gave of your time and advice. Thank you.

Emmanuel Wasake jr
You dove into this project with such enthusiasm and dedication, propelling me
to the finish line. Thank you for keeping up with the odd hours.

Maria Mahoro
Thank you for being my fresh set of eyes, and for unwaveringly believing in me, always.

Rachel Magoola
Thank your for your quick, invaluable advice.

Carol Waldmann, MD
Your constancy, reliability and friendship enabled me to write this book. I thank you.

Jackson
Thank you for your advice.

Dr. Charles Mulekwa
For your time, critical advice and encouragement. Thank you.

Zachary
Thank you

'We make a living by what we get. We make a life by what we give.'
Sir Winston Churchill

Global Vllage Children's Project, Inc
www.gvOrphans.org

VOCABULARY

English into Lusoga [Loo So Gah]

English	Lusoga	Pronunciation	English	Lusoga	Pronunciation
Baby	Omwana	[Oh Mwah Nah]	Snake	Omusota	[Oh Moo So Tar]
Butterflies	Ebiwoiwolo	[Eh bee woi woe lo]	Garden	Enimiro	[Eh Nee Me Row]
Bride	Omugole	[Oh Moo Go Lay]	Maize/Corn	Duuma	[Doo Ma]
Caterpillar	Ekigumbulizi	[Eh Chi Goombu Lee Zee]	Potatoes	Embooli	[Em Bo Lee]
Dress	Ekiteteyi	[Eh Chi Teh Teh Yee]	Cassava	Muwogo	[Moo War Go]
Home	Waka	[Wah Kar]	Banana Trees	Ebigogo	[Eh Bee Go Go]
School	Eisomelo	[Ei So Me Lo]	Bananas	Amenvu	[Ah Menvoo]
Shoes	Engaito	[En Guy Toe]	Mango	Omuyembe	[Oh Moo Yembe]
Sun	Endhuba	[En Doo Bar]	Guavas	Amapeera	[Ah Ma Pera]
Neighbor	Muliranwa	[Moo Lee Rah Nwah]	Orange	Omukyungwa	[O Moo Choongwa]
Tree	Omuti	[Oh Moo Tee]	Lemon	Eniimu	[Eh Nee Moo]
Moon	Omwezi	[Oh Mweh Zee]	House	Enhumba	[Eh Noomba]
Electricity	Amasanhalaze	[Ah Mah SaNaLa Zey]	Firewood	Enku	[Ehn Coo]
Mum	Maama	[Maama]	Water	Amadhi	[Ah Mar Dee]
Dad	Baaba	[Baaba]	Digging	Okulima	[Oh Coo Lee Mah]
Reed Mat	Ekisampa	[Eh Chee Sampa]	Chores	Emirimu	[Eh Me Ree Moo]

Part 1

[Kisa means grace]

While she was growing up, Kisa was a very happy child. She smiled and laughed all the time. And when she was sad, she cried. But she smiled and laughed more than she cried because her family loved her very much.

Her skin and eyes were brown like the beautiful earth on which she played. Together, Kisa and her family lived in a small house built out of mud and clay. The roof was made out of logs and wood and iron sheets.

When it rained, the sound of the raindrops falling on the roof was very loud, and sometimes when the thunder roared, Kisa was afraid. But she did not show it because the lovely smell of the earth filled their house and she'd just close her eyes and breathe it in.

Her mother liked to say Kisa started singing before she could talk; and started dancing before she could walk. Kisa believed this to be true. She danced to the music coming out of their small radio. If that was not on, she sang to herself, clapped her hands and danced!

Kisa had 5 brothers and 7 sisters. They all lived with their parents and enjoyed being with one another by singing, dancing and telling stories. When they wanted Kisa to dance for them, they'd all sing:

'Kisa, Kisa, Kisa nabugere butono aselengeta;
[Kisa, Kisa, Kisa with the tiny feet is slipping & sliding down the hill]

Kisa tiyaidha kumbona,
Kisa nabugere butono aselengeta.'
[Kisa did not come to see me,
Kisa with the tiny feet is slipping & sliding down the hill]

She would then stand on tiptoe and dance up and down and she would laugh!

The family had a dog named Tannaziraba; but every one called him Tanna. Kisa had full conversations with Tanna; and she sometimes also talked to herself.
[Tannaziraba means 'Has not yet lived a hard life.']

3

Kisa's family all ate their lunch together.
Her brothers and sisters and mother sat on reed mats
under the big mango tree in their compound.

Her father sat on a chair and his food was
placed on a small stool.

Starting with the youngest child, their mother served
the food in appropriate portions onto everyone's plate
before they each picked their food up; and then her
mother served her father last before she sat down to eat.

One by one, as they finished eating,
they thanked their mother for cooking, then thanked
their father for providing for the family.

Kisa's father would then thank her mother for
the food and her mother thanked him back for
providing for them all.

4

5

In the evening, when the sun was going down, Kisa and her family listened to the news on the radio before they sat inside the house to eat supper with light coming from kerosene lamps.

6

The glow from the lamps made everyone's face bright and this always made Kisa feel warm inside. They ate in the same way they did at lunch. However, sometimes after supper, her father took out his flute and played a song they all knew very well.

After that, when everyone was ready to go to bed, Kisa's father made sure that all lamps except his were blown out and that all the children were in bed. Then, he'd go to make sure that both the front and back doors were locked properly.

When that was done, Kisa would hear him get into bed, put the keys under his pillow before blowing out his lamp. Kisa always wished him goodnight before she fell asleep feeling very safe in their home.

Part 2

Kisa was a very respectful and obedient child. Although she loved to play with her friends, she always stopped playing and immediately ran to either her mother, father or whoever else called for her.

When her parents needed sugar, salt or soap from the shops nearby, they called for her, gave her the money and sent her running all the way there and back.

Because she was always eager to go and also because she was a fast runner, Kisa's parents always preferred to send her.

If Kisa had to buy a number of things, she did not write them down on a paper. Instead, she made the items into a song and sang this all the way to the shops.

Every morning, Kisa and her brothers and sisters took turns to help around the house.

They washed the dishes, swept and cleaned the house and then they all gathered twigs and logs for firewood so their mother could cook their food over a pit fire.

In the afternoon, Kisa and the others went to the well to fetch water for drinking, cooking and bathing.

On the way back from the well, Kisa proudly balanced a pot full of water on her head without using her hands while chatting with everyone. She'd learned this from her sisters and her friends.

'The sooner I finish my chores, the sooner I can go back to play,' Kisa would tell herself while she worked.

11

12

Kisa's mother had a garden in which she grew potatoes, tomatoes, beans and other food. Sometimes, she took Kisa with her. But Kisa did not like to dig. This was not because she was lazy. She was just very afraid of the caterpillars that were everywhere in the garden.

'Argh, how scary these caterpillars are,' she'd say to Tanna. 'Mama says they won't eat me though.'

Kisa's teacher said caterpillars turned into beautiful butterflies and this made Kisa a little less scared.

Besides, Tanna was always close by to protect her from the caterpillars while he tried to catch butterflies.

'Mama says if I don't learn to dig for food,
I won't be able to feed my family when I grow up!'

One day while playing hide and seek with her little sister, Kisa put her middle finger in the door hinge and without knowing, her sister closed the door on it, almost tearing it's tip off.

Kisa did not scream or panic. Although she was in pain, she thought not to scare her little sister and calmly asked her to open the door so she could get her finger out.

At first, her sister thought Kisa was joking. But when she saw the blood, she panicked, quickly opened the door and started to cry after realizing she'd hurt her beloved sister.

Part 3

After wrapping her finger to stop the bleeding, their father put her on the back of his bicycle; and together, they rode all the way to the hospital, which was far from their home.

Although Kisa was in pain, she did not cry because her father told her it was going to be alright. She held on all the way.

At the hospital, the doctor took the wrap off, cleaned the finger and stitched it. He smiled at her while doing this and she was not afraid anymore.

On the way home, her father bought her soda and cake because she was a brave little girl.

Sometimes, after doing her chores, Kisa played a tap and run game called *tapo* or a ballgame, *nobo,* with the other girls.

Other times, the children, both boys and girls, went on adventures through the gardens of maize, sweet potatoes, groundnuts, cassava, bananas, mangoes, avocados, guavas, oranges, lemons; jack fruit.

They climbed trees for ripe mangoes and guavas even when these trees were in a neighbor's yard. The air filled with sweetness when the fruit was ready.

The children also built tents out of bed sheets under the big mango tree and played house. They also threw parties and put on weddings.

20

Kisa put make up on the bride's face using the powder from crushed bricks and the lipstick was from red flowers.

With her friends, she also made dolls from the almost dry banana stalks. The stalks were laid across one another and wrapped over and over a few times to make the head. Then, she made arms and legs.

She sewed her dolls' clothes from small pieces of cloth her mother gave her. Sometimes, the needle pricked her finger. When this happened, her sister helped with the sewing.

Kisa also made balls from wrapping the fiber round and round, until her ball was perfect.

The school term always started on a Monday morning. Kisa's mother got her up, made sure she took a bath, ate her breakfast; and wore her school uniform.

This was a red dress with a stiff belt and sometimes, she had a new pair of shoes.

Kisa left the house with Tanna at her side for part of the way. The neighbor's yard had an olive tree; and if she was lucky, there were a few olives on the ground for her to pick and put into her uniform dress pocket for a snack later.

She couldn't trust the school bag her mother made for her with the precious olives because it always lost small pencils and erasers.

'I need to go meet my friends now,' she'd tell Tanna before he went home.

Part 4

Having spent her days away from school free and barefoot, Kisa found it hard to spend whole days at school wearing shoes. They hurt her feet. So, when she got to school, she took them off and gave them to her teacher who, in turn, gave them back to her at the end of the day. She carried them all the way home.

On their way from school, Kisa and her friends sang:

'Ffe tuli embaata ento,

['We are little ducklings,]

Tetumanyi kubala,

[We don't know how to count,]

Tubala nga tuddamu,

[We count while repeating,]

Emu, bbiri, ssattu, nnya ...'

[One, two, three, four ...']

On the weekend, her father brought out his small blackboard and chalk to teach her math, English and other subjects. Her father taught her a new word that sounded like KAN - TAN - KARAS.

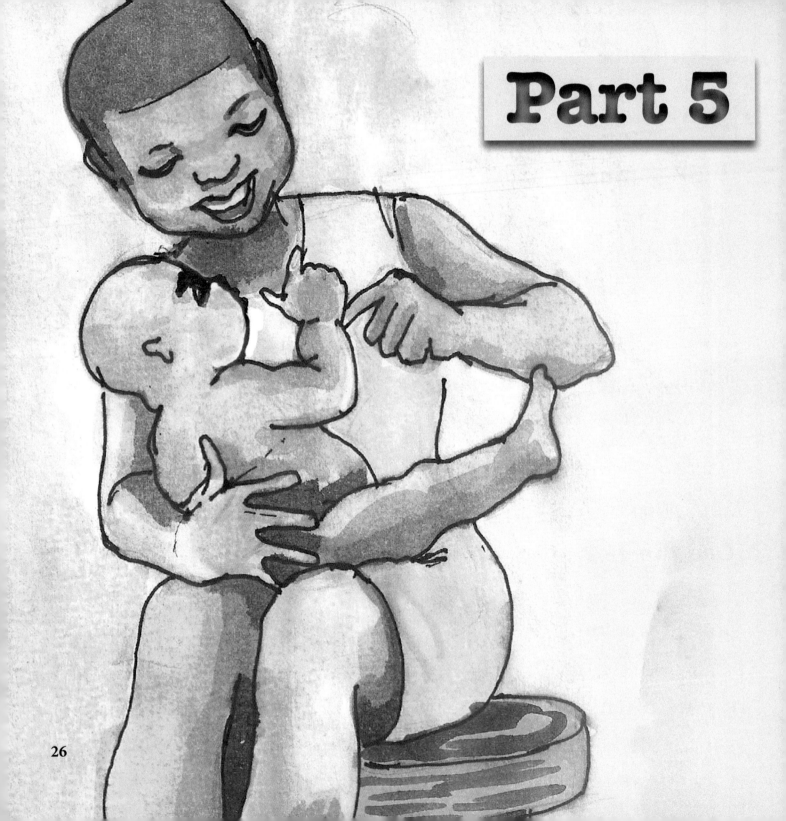

Part 5

One day her mother went to town with her Uncle's wife and did not come back until the next day.

When the two women came back, her mother was carrying a baby girl. She told Kisa that they had found the baby in a rubbish bin and had had no choice but to bring her home.

Kisa was puzzled at first; but after looking at the beautiful baby, she knew her mother could not help herself.

Then one by one the neighbours came by to see and bless the new baby. Kisa could not have been more excited. 'Mama says when the baby is a little older, I can help bathe, feed and teach her new things,' She told Tanna.

One of the neighbours was Aunt Alice. When she came to see the new baby she was so excited that she started to dance and sing to celebrate the newest member of the tribe:

'Abasoga twesiimye n'ensi Busoga,
[We, the Basoga people, are proud of our Nation of Busoga]

Yakitalo era yakyewunhio. Abasoga twesiimye n'ensi Busoga
[It's just marvelous. We Basoga are proud of our Nation Busoga,]

Ekulukuta amata n'omubisi ogwendhuki!'
[For it flows with milk and honey!]

As her baby sister grew older, Kisa never forgot how her sister had been saved. And each time the child destroyed Kisa's toys or pinched her, she told her that she'd ask their mother to take her back to the bin she was saved from.

When their mother and the older children heard this, they smiled knowingly.

Holidays came three times a year for Kisa. But she liked the Christmas holidays the most. Kisa's father bought her mother cloth to make a new *gomesi*.

Although this dress required a lot of fabric to make, there was always some left over.

From this, her mother made Kisa a Christmas dress too. Her mother made both dresses on a very old sewing machine. If Kisa was among the top three pupils at the end of the school year, she'd also get new shoes if her father had the money.

Kisa especially liked Christmas eve when the moon was up and it lit up every one's face. Kisa's father sang bass and she thought he had the best voice in the whole world. They sang in the moonlight before going to bed.

Part 6

When Kisa's family awoke on Christmas morning, breakfast was lots and lots of treats they didn't eat all year round: bread & butter, *mandazi, chapati, samosa.*

After that, the whole family in their best clothes walked to church with their mother and father at the front. Wearing the same fabric as her mother made Kisa feel so special.

32

33

Church service was usually over in the very early afternoon and Kisa's family came home to a very big, and very delicious lunch.

This was the only time of the year when Kisa was allowed to eat all the meat she wanted and all the soda she could drink. Save for weddings and parties, it was at Christmas that Kisa would eat cake too!

Tanna and his neighborhood dog friends also ate as much meat as they could and gnawed at the bones. Soon, it's the New Year. All the meat has been eaten, all the soda drunk.

'I hope you had a good Christmas with all the meat and bones, Tanna,' Kisa said. 'School begins again in a few days.'

Before she went to bed, Kisa knelt beside her bed and prayed. She thanked God for Christmas, the new dress and all the good food. She asked Him to watch over her and the whole family while they were asleep.

When she got into bed, she heard her father locking the doors. As she drifted off to sleep, Kisa was already looking forward to the next Christmas when she'd eat meat, cake and drink lots of soda.

'Good night Tanna. God bless mum and dad. God bless my sisters - Rose, Joy, Robinah, Jane, Sarah, Winnie and Esther. God, please bless my brothers Henry, Bob, Michael, Dan, Emma.'

Then she said 'Good night' to her father. In response, and as a special treat, her father played a few bars of his favorite song on the flute, soothing her and the rest of the family ever so gently to sleep.